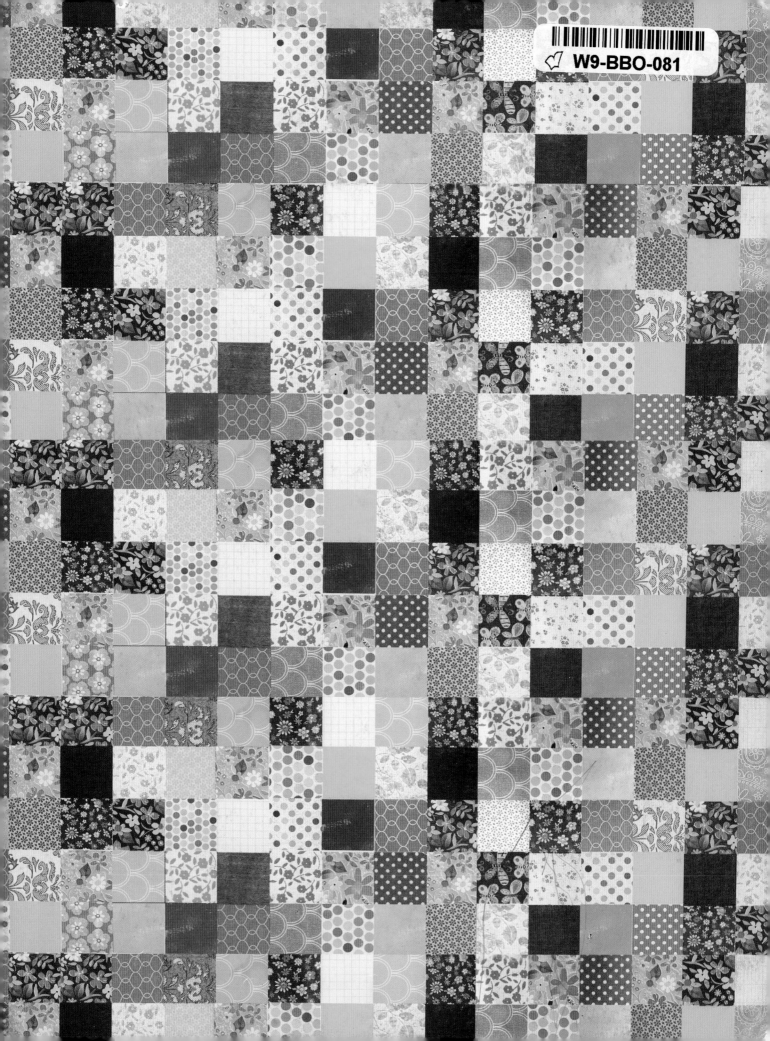

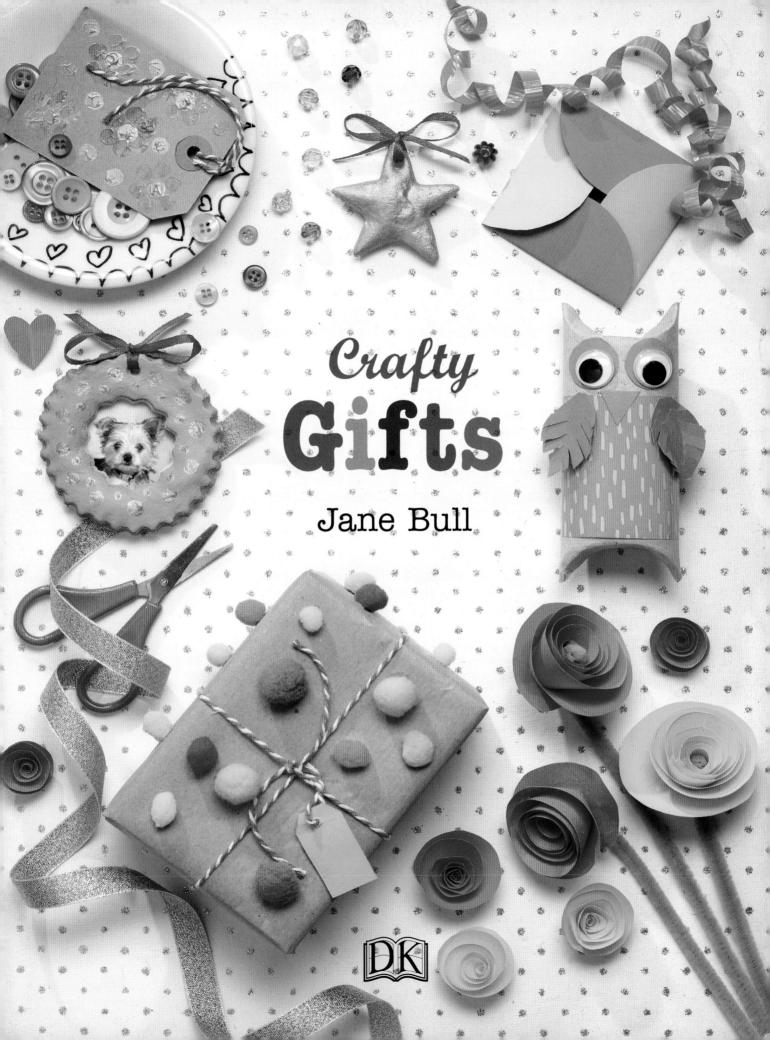

Crafty
Gifts

Jane Bull

DK

Design and text Jane Bull
Photographer Andy Crawford
Editor Violet Peto
US Editor Margaret Parrish
Design Assistant Eleanor Bates
Producer, Pre-Production Nikoleta Parasaki
Producer John Casey
Jacket Designer Amy Keast
Jacket Coordinator Francesca Young
Managing Editor Penny Smith
Managing Art Editor Mabel Chan
Publisher Mary Ling
Art Director Jane Bull

This book is for my sister
Margaret

First American Edition, 2017
Published in the United States by DK Publishing
345 Hudson Street, New York, New York 10014

Copyright © 2017 Dorling Kindersley Limited
DK, a Division of Penguin Random House LLC
17 18 19 20 21 10 9 8 7 6 5 4 3 2 1
001–297035–Oct/2017

Published in Great Britain by Dorling Kindersley Limited.

A catalog record for this book is available from
the Library of Congress.
ISBN: 978-1-4654-6122-3

DK books are available at special discounts when purchased
in bulk for sales promotions, premiums, fund-raising, or
educational use. For details, contact: DK Publishing Special
Markets, 345 Hudson Street, New York, New York 10014
SpecialSales@dk.com

Printed and bound in China

A WORLD OF IDEAS:
SEE ALL THERE IS TO KNOW

www.dk.com

Safety
Projects in this book may require adult supervision.
**When you see the warning triangle, take extra
care and ask an adult for help.**

Contents

Crafty kit 8

Crafty gift ideas

Crafty cards

Crafty gift wrap

Crafty kit

It's good to be prepared, so keep these items on hand. You will need them for most of the projects that follow. Additional materials you will need are suggested throughout the book.

Glue stick

For paper and card stock

Scissors

Tape

Strong glue

An all-purpose strong glue will stick to fabric and plastic.

Felt-tip pen

Colorful paper and card stock

Pencil

Ruler

Crafty
gift ideas

Gems

Beads and
buttons

Snowman

Festive
trees

Santa

Tiny jingle
bells

You will need:

Sewing needle
with large eye
and blunt end

Thick cotton
thread

12in (30cm)

Button charms

These colorful gems make perfect gifts at festive times. Enjoy them hanging on the Christmas tree or sparkling against a sunny window.

1
Thread the needle and pass it through the buttons and beads.

2
Then pass the needle back through a different hole.

3
Make the threads equal lengths and knot the ends together.

Icicle

Mix up the buttons and beads to create different colorways and dangly shapes.

Salt dough treasures

Make fancy decorations, colorful frames, and gift tags using salt dough. Shape it, bake it, and paint it for a luscious finish, and transform simple salt dough into these special presents.

You will need:

2½ cups
all-purpose flour

+

⅓ cup salt

+

1 tsp vegetable oil

+

1 cup
water

=

Make some dough

Pour all the ingredients into a mixing bowl. Mix them together with your hands until the dough forms a ball.

You will need:

Candleholders

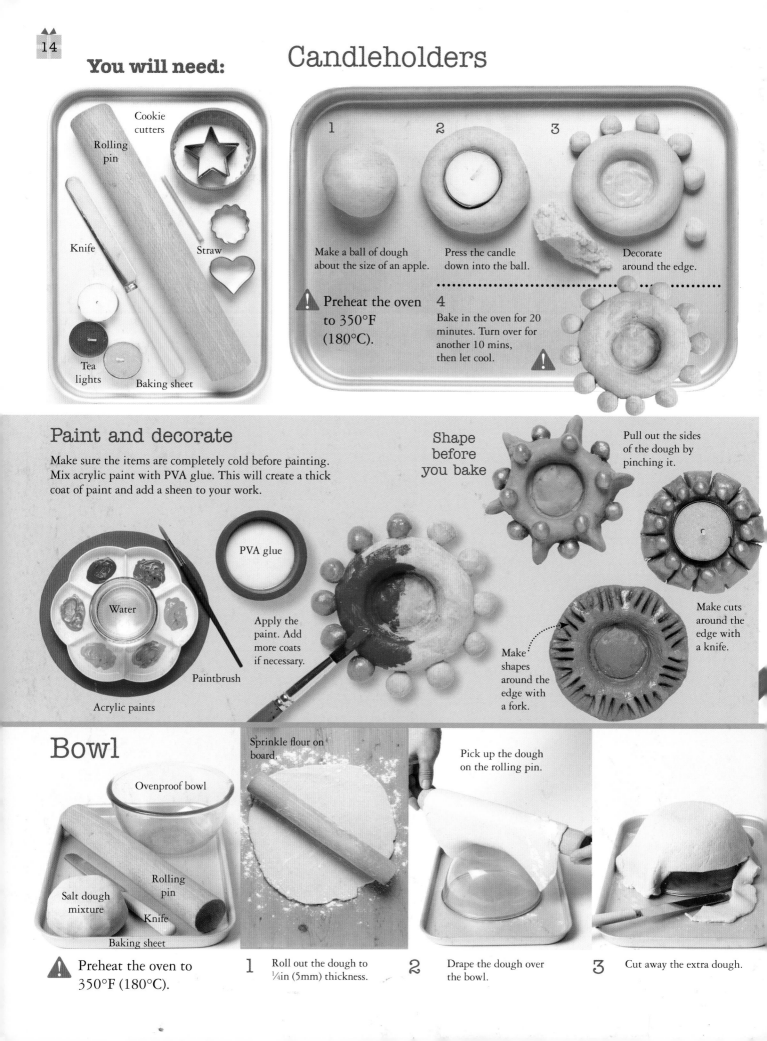

Cookie cutters

Rolling pin

Knife

Straw

Tea lights

Baking sheet

1 Make a ball of dough about the size of an apple.

2 Press the candle down into the ball.

3 Decorate around the edge.

⚠ Preheat the oven to 350°F (180°C).

4 Bake in the oven for 20 minutes. Turn over for another 10 mins, then let cool. ⚠

Paint and decorate

Make sure the items are completely cold before painting. Mix acrylic paint with PVA glue. This will create a thick coat of paint and add a sheen to your work.

Shape before you bake

Pull out the sides of the dough by pinching it.

PVA glue

Water

Paintbrush

Acrylic paints

Apply the paint. Add more coats if necessary.

Make shapes around the edge with a fork.

Make cuts around the edge with a knife.

Bowl

Ovenproof bowl

Rolling pin

Salt dough mixture

Knife

Baking sheet

⚠ Preheat the oven to 350°F (180°C).

Sprinkle flour on board.

1 Roll out the dough to ¼in (5mm) thickness.

Pick up the dough on the rolling pin.

2 Drape the dough over the bowl.

3 Cut away the extra dough.

Decorations

Preheat the oven to 350°F (180°C).

1 Roll out the dough to ¼in (5mm) thickness.

2

3 Place the shape onto the baking sheet and cut out the middle.

Take out the center shape and place on the sheet. Use the straw to make the holes.

4 Bake in the oven for 15 minutes. Then let cool.

Baking tips:

• Preheat the oven before baking.

• Make the dough shapes directly on the baking sheet because they may become misshapen if moved.

• You may need to bake for longer to ensure that the dough is fully dried out.

Paint the decorations. Let dry and add other colors.

For extra decoration, you will also need:
• photo
• ribbon

Add a photo

1 Place the decoration over the photo. Draw around the edge.

2 Cut out the photo, making it a bit smaller than the outer edge.

3 Spread glue on the back of the decoration and position the photo.

Let the glue dry, then attach ribbons.

Bake in the oven for 25 minutes, or until the dough has dried out.

4 Roll out a sausage shape with the extra dough. Place the sausage on the base of the bowl.

5 Let cool before painting.

6 Paint inside and outside the bowl. Let dry and paint on colorful patterns.

Apple packs

Make a great crop of crafty gifts from recycled plastic bottles. Choose any size or color and transform them into these clever, apple-shaped containers.

A treat just for you X

How to make an apple pack

You will need:

- two plastic bottles • some goodies to pack inside
- green or red tissue paper • ribbon • scissors
- green and brown paper • pencil • strong glue

A clear bottle with a red tissue-paper apple

1 Cut here.

2 Wrap up your gift in green or red tissue paper.

3 Place the gift in one bottle base.

4 Push the two bottle bases together.

Glue on ribbon to decorate.

5 Cut out leaves in different sizes.

Glue a large leaf on first.

Then glue the base of the stalk on top.

6 Next, make the stalk and add the leaves.

Cut a strip of brown paper 4in x ¾in (10cm x 1½cm) for the stalk.

Fold twice to make a base.

Put glue on both ends.

Glue the two ends together with a leaf in between.

18

DIY gingerbread folk

This clever kit makes a great gift for a favorite cook who loves to bake. Pack the ingredients in a fancy jar, then attach a cookie cutter and instructions on how to make these delicious gingerbread treats.

You will need:

• Spoon • Clean paper

1⅔ cups all-purpose flour

1 tsp ground ginger and 1 tsp pumpkin pie spice

1 tsp baking soda

A clean 1-quart (1-liter) jar with a lid

Ribbon

Gingerbread cookie cutter and card tag (with instructions on the back)

⅔ cup dark brown sugar

Plastic bag of candy-coated chocolates for decoration

Plastic bag for confectioners' sugar

¾ cup confectioners' sugar

How to fill the jar

1 Spoon in the flour and baking soda.

Make a paper funnel to stop the flour from spilling.

2 Add sugar, then spice.

Press each layer down with the back of a spoon.

3 Add a bag of confectioners' sugar.

This way the sugar won't get mixed up with the other ingredients.

4 Screw on the lid.

Add a bag of candy to decorate the cookies.

Instructions

Write the instructions on a card and attach it to the jar.

How to bake your cookies

Makes: 18 gingerbread folk
You will also need:
• 7 tbsp butter • 1 egg
• 2 tbsp golden syrup or corn syrup
For the icing: lemon juice
Equipment: mixing bowl, wooden spoon, plastic wrap, rolling pin, baking sheet, small bowl, cooling rack, piping bag.

⚠ Start baking

1. Preheat the oven to 350°F (180°C).
2. In a mixing bowl, add softened butter, egg, and syrup. Beat together with a wooden spoon until creamy.
3. Add the dry ingredients from the jar (except the candies and confectioners' sugar) and combine well.
4. Use your hands to make the mixture into a ball. Wrap in plastic wrap and leave in the fridge for 30 mins.
5. Roll out the mixture to ¼in (5mm) thickness. Cut out the cookies and place them on the baking sheet.
6. Put in the oven and bake for 15 mins. Take out and let cool on a rack.
7. Decorate with icing and candies.

FOR THE ICING
1. Put the confectioners' sugar into a small bowl and add the lemon juice. Mix together and add a little water if too stiff.
2. Put into a piping bag ready to decorate.

Jars of goodies

for Doodlers

Make a giant pencil packed with all a doodler needs to get creative.

Cut out a circle from brown kraft paper. Fold it into a cone to fit the top of the lid (see page 61).

Color in the top of the pencil.

Glue to the lid with strong glue.

for A sweetie

Dress up two jars and fill them with someone's favorite treats.

Make a happy hat from an old glove (see page 60).

Glue on wobbly eyes, a button nose, and a salt-dough smile.

Cut off the cuff and two fingers of an old glove. Sew them together to make a cozy scarf.

You will need:

- Clean glass (or good quality plastic) jars with screw-on lids

Find out more about decorating the jars on page 60.

for Crafty crafters

Here's a sewing kit for budding stitchers. They'll have all they need in one place, topped off with a pincushion.

Create a pincushion from a two-part lid (see page 60).

for Cookie cooks

Not only does this cookie jar contain ingredients and instructions for making delicious cookies, but it also serves as a cookie container!

Ingredients:

1 cup brown sugar
1¾ cups all-purpose flour
1 tsp baking soda
5½oz (150g) candy-coated chocolates
(in a plastic bag)

Fill the jar using the same method as on page 19.

Make a fancy label and write out the baking instructions (see page 60).

Bathtime fizz

These bath fizzes are full of fizzy fun!

Watch them explode with delicious flowery scents as they
melt in the bathwater. They're the perfect gift for anyone
who deserves a relaxing time.

A treat just
for **YOU**
x

Sugar cake
decorations will
melt away in
the bath.

How to make a bath fizz

The basic recipe contains baking soda, citric acid powder, oil, and water. You can change the color, smell, decoration, and shape to suit the lucky recipient of your gift.

Lavender scented fizzies
You will need:

Blue food coloring

Lavender scented oil

1¼ cups citric acid powder

Sugar stars

2 tsp olive oil

1 cup baking soda

Water sprayer

- large mixing bowl • teaspoon
- large spoon for mixing
- ice-cube tray to make the shapes

1

Citric acid

Baking soda

Olive oil

Combine the three ingredients (as shown) in the mixing bowl.

Mix it up

2

Food coloring

Stir the color into the mixture.

Add some color

3

Scented oil

Other scented oils to try: vanilla, peppermint, and orange.

Pour in about 10 drops of scented oil and mix well.

Add some nice smells

4

Spray about 7 squirts of water and mix in well.

Add water

5

The mixture is ready when it clumps together.

Squeeze it together with your hands. ....

Shape the bath fizzies

Use a clean, dry ice-cube tray or similar mold.

1

Sprinkle sugar-star decorations into the shapes.

Ice-cube tray with heart shapes

2

Spoon in the mixture. Press it down and keep filling.

3

Firmly press down the mixture into the mold.

4

Let set for 2 hours, then pop out the fizzies.

Fill a clean, dry, air-tight jar.

Ready to gift wrap

Use within one month to make the most of the smells.

More fizzy ideas

Use the same basic mix, but try out different scented oils or decorations. You can also use other molds, such as cupcake pans.

Refreshing ice

You will need:
- ice-cube tray
- basic fizzy mix
- peppermint scented oil
- sparkly cake decorations

Tangy citrus cupcakes

You will need:
- cupcake pan
- basic fizzy mix
- orange scented oil
- sugar cake decorations

Picture it!

Create a work of art for a special person. Draw a simple design
and fill in the shape to create a gem of a picture.

Buttons,
beads, and
googly
eyes

You will need:

Picture frame:
about 8in x 8in
(20cm x 20cm)
is a good size

White paper

Thin card stock

Strong glue

Scissors

Pencil

1 Draw a simple shape on
paper and cut it out.

Place the paper shape
on the card stock and
trace around it.

2 Cut out the card stock shape
and position it on a piece of
paper that fits your frame.
Lightly draw around the shape.

3

Spread glue
inside the
shape.

Glue on googly eyes, then,
starting at the edge, add
buttons and beads. Soon your
picture will be ready to frame!

You're a star!

Use a mini canvas for a pocket-sized picture.

Use felt-tip pens to add details to your design.

This belongs to...

Make your favorite people feel special with their very own decorated ceramics. This mug for Mom will be perfect for her well-earned coffee breaks.

You can add a treat, too. Wrap it in a pretty bag tied with a ribbon.

You're all heart

Draw a picture or doodle some simple patterns.

Purr-fect for cat lovers

A matching cat plate

You will need:

- plain, glazed ceramics
- ceramic markers • scissors • paper
- double-sided tape or stickers

You can use any plain, glazed ceramics, such as cups, saucers, mugs, plates, or bowls.

Mom

Making pictures

1

Try out some designs first with pen and paper— just doodle!

2

Draw your design directly onto the ceramic surface.

3

Color in your design, add a name, then let dry.

Mom

Scribbles and dots

1

Use stickers or paper stuck to double-sided tape.

Cut out a shape.

2

Glue your shape on the mug. Draw some scribbles or dots.

3

Let dry, then peel off the shape.

Write a message.

You're the best!

To fix your design:

⚠ 1. Place the dry items on an ovenproof tray.
2. Place the tray on the middle shelf in a COLD oven.
3. Heat the oven to 325°F (160°C).
4. Bake for 30 minutes, then turn off the oven.
5. LET THE ITEMS COOL DOWN.
6. Remove them from the oven when cold.

NOTE: Follow the manufacturer's instructions given with your pens.

Not sure about drawing a picture? Then use a sticker shape and scribble over it (see instructions on the previous page).

Super Hero!

Dad

Best Teacher

Make a pincushion. Wrap fabric around soft stuffing, then glue the cushion into an eggcup.

Eggheads

Make a gift set

Once you are happy with your design, apply it to different ceramic things to create a collection, such as a mug with a matching coaster and plate.

We're dotty about you

You're the best!

Top tile coasters

Mom

You're the best!

Decorate plain ceramic tiles and heat in the same way as the plates and cups.

Thanks a bunch

Paper roses are as pretty as the real ones, but by using paper petals and fuzzy pipe cleaners, there are no prickly thorns!

You will need:

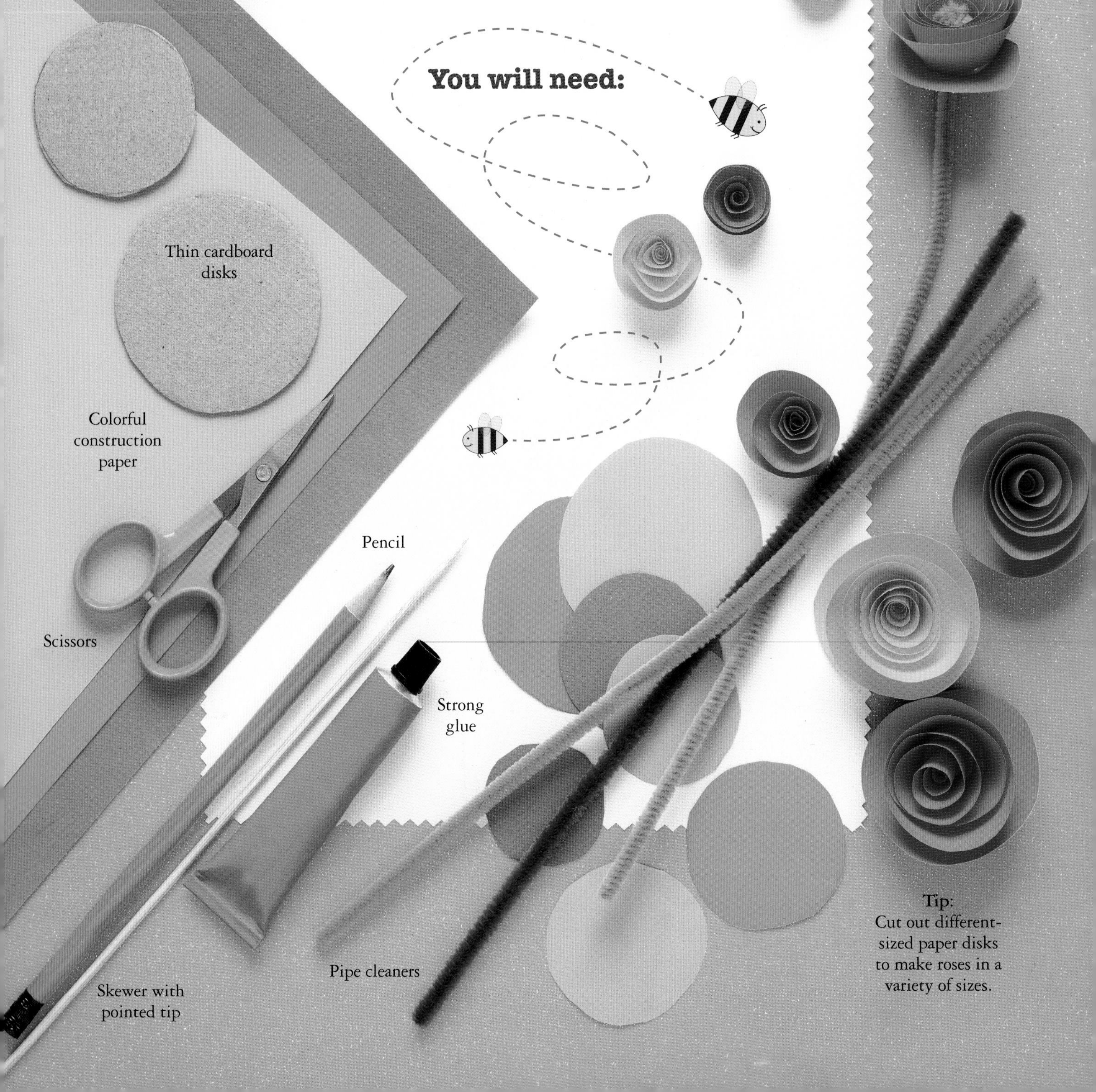

Thin cardboard disks

Colorful construction paper

Scissors

Pencil

Strong glue

Skewer with pointed tip

Pipe cleaners

Tip: Cut out different-sized paper disks to make roses in a variety of sizes.

Everything's coming up roses!

Make them match

For the perfect matching gift set, make smaller roses and glue them onto a greeting card, a gift tag, and wrapping paper.

How to make a rose

1 Cut out a paper disk

Place a cardboard disk on the colored paper. Draw around it with a pencil. Cut out the paper disk.

2 Turn the disk into a spiral

Draw a spiral on the paper disk, then cut it out.

Roll up at the outer end of the spiral.

Roll around the skewer.

Let the spiral open out slightly.

Glue the inner, flat end.

Stick the flat end and the coiled paper together.

3 Roll it up

4 Glue in place

Bend the tip of the pipe cleaner over to hold it in place.

Make a hole with a skewer through the base of the rose.

Insert the pipe cleaner through the hole to make the stalk.

5 Make a hole

6 Insert the stalk

Lovebugs

Special greetings

are brought to you on the backs of these cute little critters. Flutter their wings to reveal the secret messages.

Glitter bug

Lovebug

Use sparkly paper and shiny sticker stars.

Ladybugs are really cute, but you can make your bugs as unique as you like. Experiment with stickers and glittery paper.

Striped bug

How to make a lovebug card

You will need:

- colorful paper for body and wings
- scissors
- eraser
- paper fastener
- glue stick
- folded greeting card
- wobbly eyes
- felt-tip pens

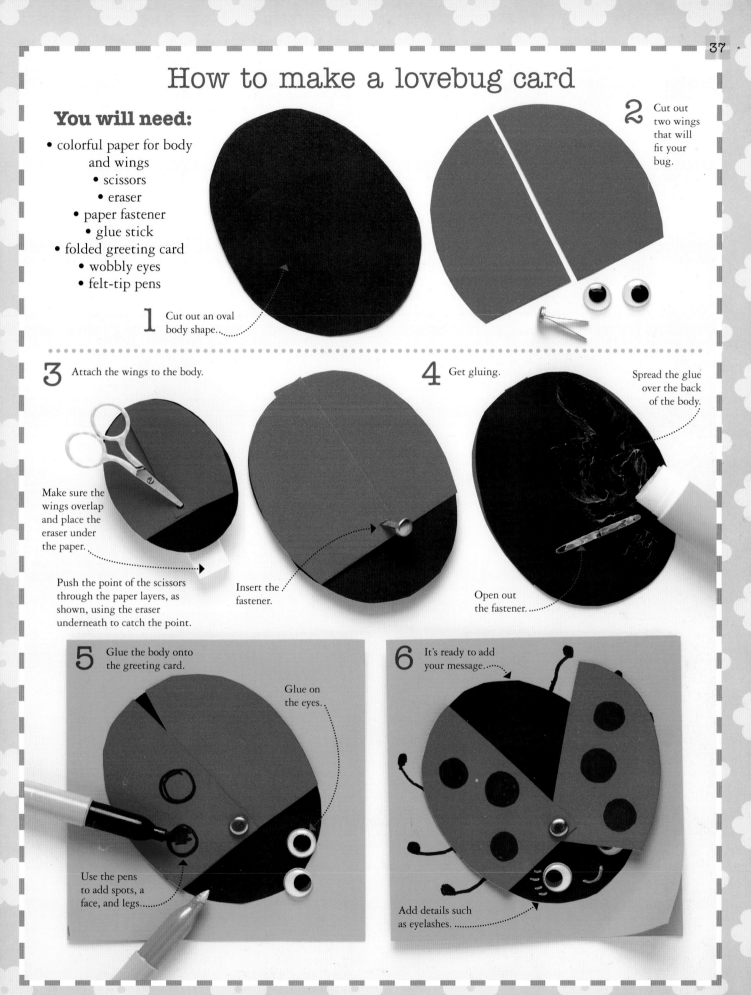

2 Cut out two wings that will fit your bug.

1 Cut out an oval body shape.

3 Attach the wings to the body.

Make sure the wings overlap and place the eraser under the paper.

Push the point of the scissors through the paper layers, as shown, using the eraser underneath to catch the point.

Insert the fastener.

4 Get gluing.

Spread the glue over the back of the body.

Open out the fastener.

5 Glue the body onto the greeting card.

Glue on the eyes.

Use the pens to add spots, a face, and legs.

6 It's ready to add your message.

Add details such as eyelashes.

Pop-up greetings

Surprise, surprise! Tell someone they're special with these pop-up bouquets, beating hearts, and stacks of gift boxes. Bring your paper pictures to life with simple 3-D effects.

Spring has sprung just for you in this gift card.

How to make cards pop

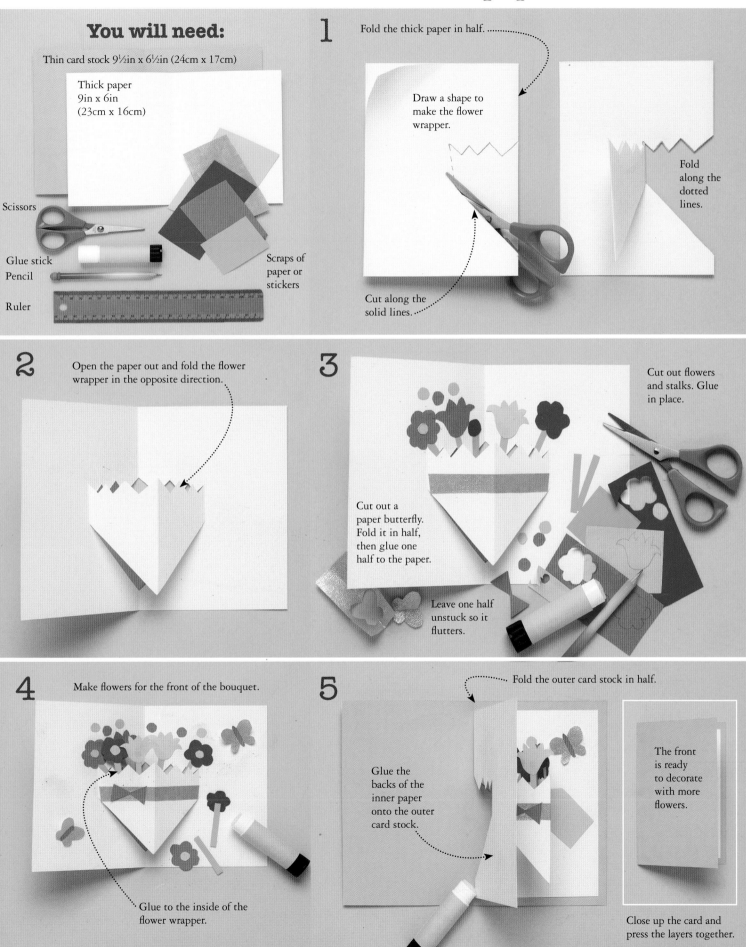

You will need:

Thin card stock 9½in x 6½in (24cm x 17cm)

Thick paper
9in x 6in
(23cm x 16cm)

Scissors

Glue stick
Pencil

Ruler

Scraps of paper or stickers

1 Fold the thick paper in half. ......

Draw a shape to make the flower wrapper.

Cut along the solid lines. ....

Fold along the dotted lines.

2 Open the paper out and fold the flower wrapper in the opposite direction.

3 Cut out flowers and stalks. Glue in place.

Cut out a paper butterfly. Fold it in half, then glue one half to the paper.

Leave one half unstuck so it flutters.

4 Make flowers for the front of the bouquet.

Glue to the inside of the flower wrapper.

5 Fold the outer card stock in half.

Glue the backs of the inner paper onto the outer card stock.

The front is ready to decorate with more flowers.

Close up the card and press the layers together.

Pop-up hearts, cakes, and gifts

Big heart

Cut along the solid lines.

Fold along the dotted lines.

Open the paper out. Fold the heart in the opposite direction.

Decorate with paper hearts.

Fold the hearts in half. Glue down one half of the smaller hearts for a 3-D effect.

Celebration cake

Cut along the solid lines.

Cut out the edge of the paper for extra decoration.

Fold along the dotted lines.

Open the paper out. Fold the cakes in the opposite direction.

Glue paper candles to the inside edge.

Glue on strips of paper for the icing.

Decorate with stickers or paper shapes.

Gifts galore

Cut along the solid lines.

Fold along the dotted lines.

Decorate the gifts with pretty paper. Cut out paper bows and glue them on.

Decorate the background with stickers or paper shapes.

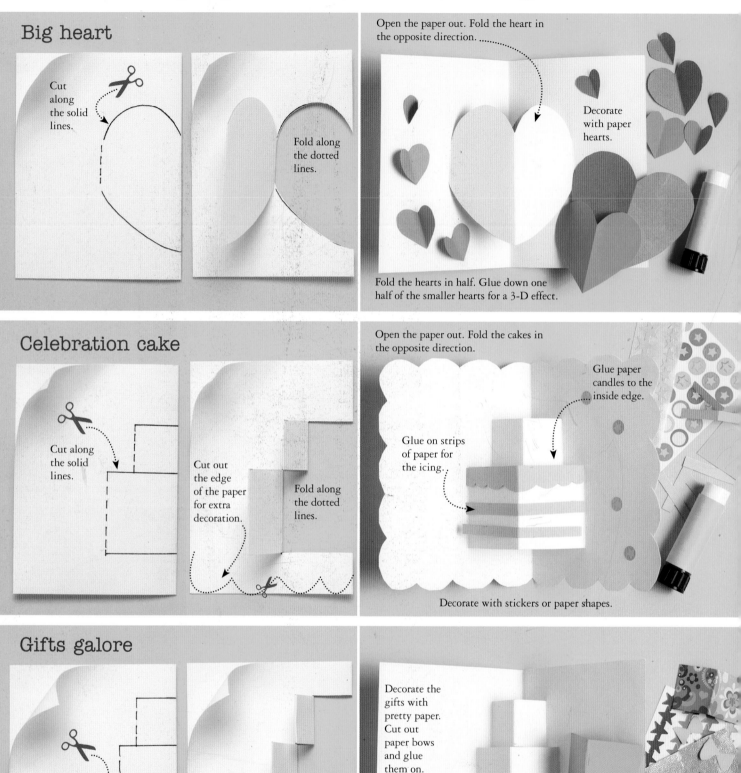

Finishing touches

Glue the inner paper and outer card stock together. Decorate the front of the card with leftover paper—a sneak preview of what's to come!

Picture perfect

The kittens arrived.

They've seen a mouse.

Choosing a new bed.

When we baked you an apple pie.

Playing ball with

We jumped on

Remember when...

Share the times you visited friends,
got a new pet, or just had fun! Make a mini album
of photos you've taken and pack them up in this clever camera card.

Memory cards

To create a camera card, glue your favorite photos to a sheet of folded paper. Stick the folded paper inside a greeting card ready for the big reveal.

You will need:

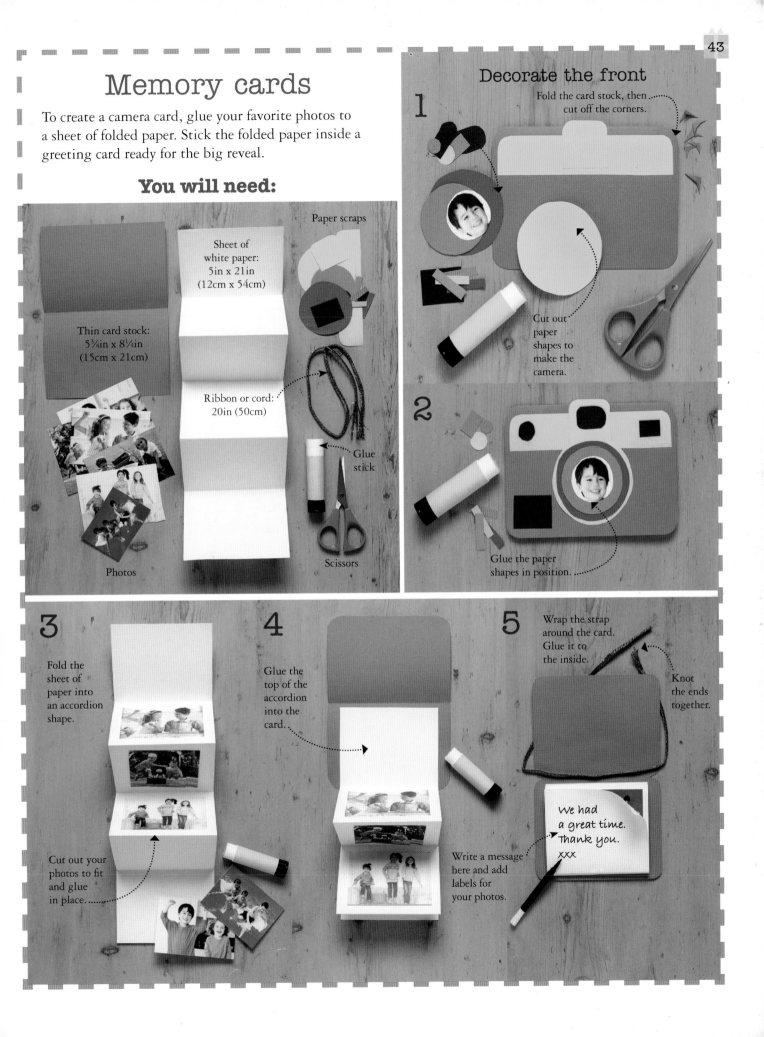

Paper scraps

Sheet of white paper: 5in x 21in (12cm x 54cm)

Thin card stock: 5¾in x 8¼in (15cm x 21cm)

Ribbon or cord: 20in (50cm)

Glue stick

Photos

Scissors

Decorate the front

1 Fold the card stock, then cut off the corners.

Cut out paper shapes to make the camera.

2 Glue the paper shapes in position.

3 Fold the sheet of paper into an accordion shape.

Cut out your photos to fit and glue in place.

4 Glue the top of the accordion into the card.

5 Wrap the strap around the card. Glue it to the inside.

Knot the ends together.

Write a message here and add labels for your photos.

We had a great time. Thank you. xxx

Cards for crafters
and hobbyists

Pack these hobby pouches with tools for a special crafter or hobbyist. They make ideal gifts for DIY experts, cooks, green-fingered gardeners, or those who love to sew.

Toolbox card

Dad

Sewing box card

Alice

You will need:

Pencil

Construction paper: 9in x 7in (22cm x 17cm)

White construction paper for tools

Felt-tip pens

Glue stick

Scissors

For the DIYers

Happy Father's Day!

Dad

Tools for the job

Draw tool shapes on white paper. Color them in, cut them out, and put them in the pouch.

Sew, it's your birthday!

Alice

For the stitchers

Write the person's name on the front and add a message under the flap.

How to make a box card

1 Fold the colored paper along the black dotted lines.

Fold the lower section inward.

2in (5cm)

2⅝in (6.5cm)

Fold the upper section inward.

Glue the edges of the bottom section only and stick to make the pocket.

2

Draw the tools with a pencil.

Go over the lines in felt-tip pen.

Cut out the tools and color them in.

3

Cut off the corners of the box.

Glue on the handle, a latch, and decorations.

Make and decorate a handle for your card.

Pack the tools into the pocket and write your greetings.

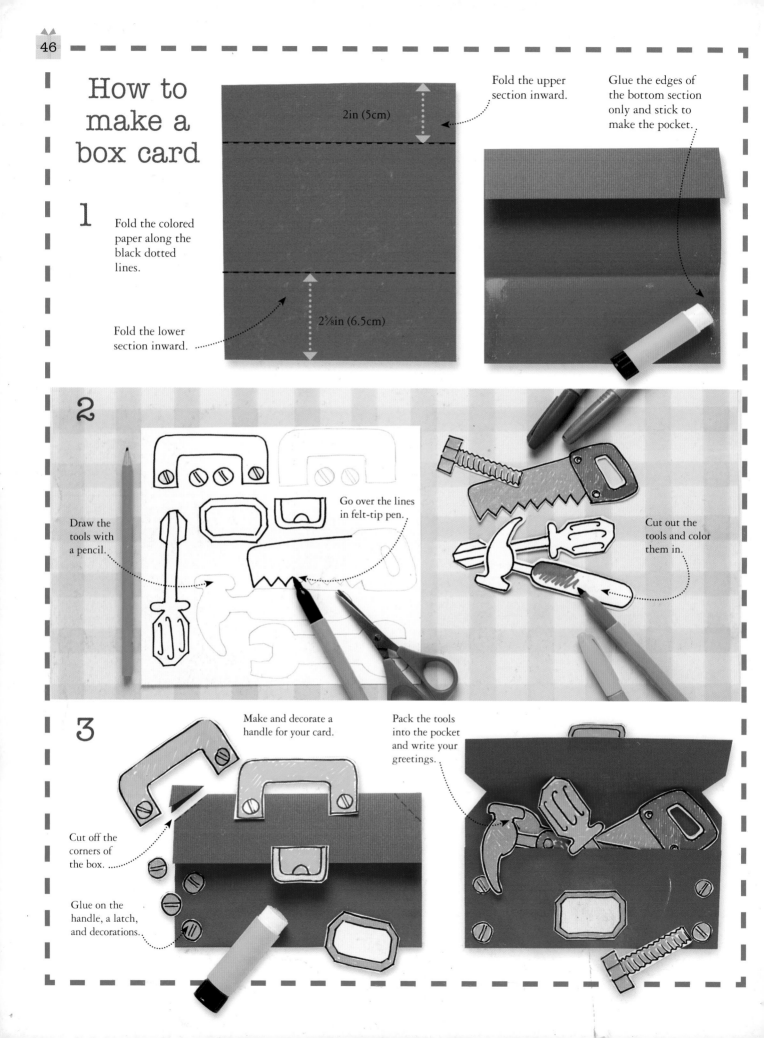

Crafty Gift Wrap

Pillow boxes

A small gift is made extra special when it is presented in a neat little gift box. It's easy to make a pillow box from a cardboard tube.

You will need:

• cardboard tube • scissors • wrapping paper or colored paper • glue stick • ribbons • googly eyes

1

Choose a cardboard tube big enough to fit your gift.

2

Fold in a side of one end of the tube.

3

Turn the tube over to fold the opposite side. Fold the other end of the tube in the same way.

4

Cut a piece of gift wrapping paper to fit around the box.

Glue along one edge of the paper and affix it to the box. Overlap with the other edge and glue in place.

5

Don't forget the gift!

Open one end of the box and insert the present. Tie a ribbon around the box to finish.

Make sure the ribbon is long enough to tie into a bow.

Alien

One googly eye is all it takes! .....

Little boxes

Decorate your boxes with leftover gift wrapping paper, colored paper, or ribbons. Or bring them to life with googly eyes.

Owl

Add paper ..... wings and a paper triangle for a beak. Finish off with big googly eyes.

For terrific trinkets

Little

There's no need to buy fancy containers when giving gifts. Make your own cheap and cheerful cartons from plain paper plates.

boxes

You will need:

• paper plate • ruler • pencil
• scissors • strong glue
• four clothespins • ribbon • stickers.

2

Fold up these pieces, then fold along the lines of the square.

Glue along one of the cut edges of the plate.

Fold and glue

4

Repeat on each corner of the square.

Let glue dry

1

Measure a square in the center of the plate. Cut along the dotted lines.

Measure and cut

3

Place the next edge against the glued edge. Hold in place with a clothespin.

Pin corner in place

5

When dry, decorate with a ribbon and stickers.

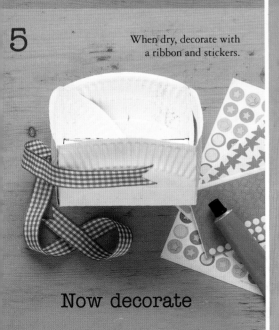

Now decorate

Stacks of gifts

Fill the boxes with homemade cookies or load them up with someone's favorite candy.

Flat packs

Wrap flat gifts such as gift tokens in these simple envelopes made from overlapping circles of colorful paper.

How to make a flat pack

You will need:

- colored paper (two different colors)
- glue stick • pencil
- scissors • ribbon

Circles and sizes

To make the circles, draw around something, such as a saucer or a lid from a jar.

Place the circular object onto the paper and draw around it.

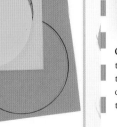

Cut out the circles. You'll need two of each color.

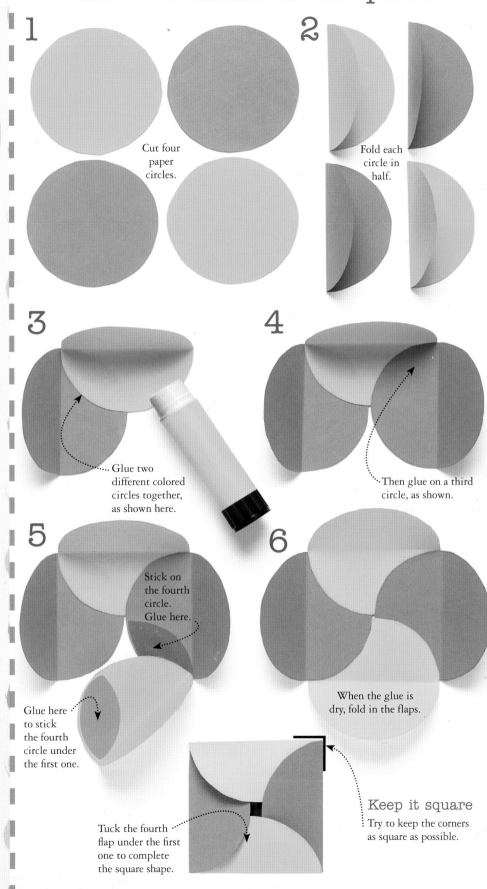

1 Cut four paper circles.

2 Fold each circle in half.

3 Glue two different colored circles together, as shown here.

4 Then glue on a third circle, as shown.

5 Stick on the fourth circle. Glue here.

Glue here to stick the fourth circle under the first one.

6 When the glue is dry, fold in the flaps.

Tuck the fourth flap under the first one to complete the square shape.

Keep it square

Try to keep the corners as square as possible.

Brown paper *packages*

Transform plain brown **kraft paper** by adding faces, stickers, and painted patterns to your packages.

The three bears

Brown boxes become Papa, Mama, and Baby Bear, with the addition of ears, wobbly eyes, and white paper muzzles (see page 59).

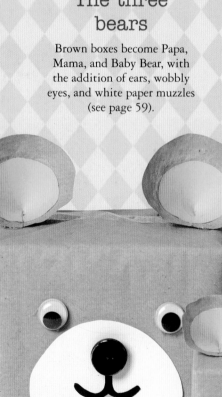

A treat just for YOU!

Dot to dotty

Polka dots and wavy line designs can be made from simple stickers.

The reindeer

Pipe cleaners bent into antler shapes turn these packages into reindeer (see page 59).

Pom-pommed

Use strong glue to attach ready-made pom-poms.

Cozy kids

Recycle snack tubes and turn them into characters with funny faces. Add wool hats made from socks or gloves (see page 60).

DIY wrapping paper

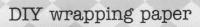

Print shop

Design your own colorful gift wrapping paper. Using household items, print shapes onto plain paper and create exotic patterns like these.

Diamonds and dots

Funny honeycomb

Crinkly circles

Luscious gold

Daisies

Latticework

You will need:

- sheets of brown paper •
tape • acrylic paint • paintbrush
- plate for paint • household items
to make prints • plain gift tags

Pencil erasers

Tape seven pencils together, making sure the ends are lined up to make an even print.

Don't forget to print matching gift tags and cards.

Plastic bag

Crumple up a plastic bag and simply press it into the paint. Then apply to the paper.

Prepare to print

Take a sheet of paper. Lay it on a flat surface and tape down the corners.

Cover the paper with the print design and let it dry before wrapping.

Pencil eraser

Single pencils make spotted designs.

Toothbrush

Cookie cutter

Dip the cutter into the paint, then press it onto the paper. Overlap the shapes to make an interlocking design.

Paint

Spread a thick layer of paint over the plate with a paintbrush. Press the items for printing into the paint, then apply them to the paper. Add more paint as needed.

Bubble wrap

Cut out a piece of bubble wrap. Press it into the paint, then apply it to the paper to print bubbles.

All wrapped up

Wrap your gifts like a professional,
then add your printed tags.

You will need:

- printed gift wrapping
  paper and gift tags
- scissors
- tape
- ribbons

Tip for a neat wrap

Don't use too much paper
or your folds will be bulky.
Use just enough to cover
your box.

1

Lay the box in the
middle of the paper.

2

Wrap the paper around
the box, folding along
the edges, as shown.

3

Overlap
the paper,
then tape it
together.

4

Fold down one
end, as shown.

5

Fold one
side in toward
the box.

6

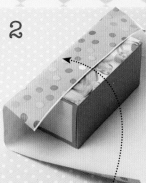

Fold the
other side in, then press
down the creases.

7

Fold the
triangular end up
and tape it in place.

8

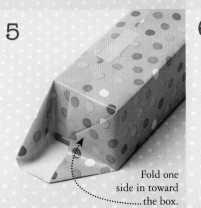

Do the same
to the other end
of the box. Add a
ribbon to finish.

Bear face

You will need:

• brown, pink, and white paper • scissors • glue stick • strong glue • googly eyes • felt-tip pen • buttons • ribbon

To make an ear, cut out a brown paper circle and a slightly smaller pink circle.

Glue the circles together with a glue stick.

Cut to the middle of the circles.

Make a cone. Glue in place with strong glue.

Leave to dry, then make the second ear.

Glue a button and a pink paper tongue to white paper to make a muzzle. Draw on a mouth.

Use strong glue to attach each ear to the top of the box.

Add googly eyes.

Glue the muzzle to the box.

Add a bow and buttons to make it look like the bear is wearing a shirt.

Ears and antlers

You will need:

• scissors • brown and pink paper • glue stick • two brown pipe cleaners • tape

Cut out a brown and a pink ear shape and glue them together.

Fold the base of the ear and glue together.

Tape an ear and an antler to each side of the box.

Bend each half backward and forward.

Fold down the tips of the antler.

Twist the antler to finish.

Bend the pipe cleaner in half.

Cozy kids
Make a beany hat from a glove.

You will need: • Wool glove • rubber band • needle and thread • pom-pom

Turn a wool glove inside out.

Gather it up with a rubber band.

Turn it right side out. (You can leave the fingers inside.)

Sew on a pom-pom.

Stretch the hat over the package and adjust to fit.

Cookie cooks
Here's how you make these delicious cookies.

Make a label for the cooking instructions.

Write the instructions here.

Makes: 20 cookies

You will also need:
• 10½ tbsp softened butter
• 1 tbsp milk

Equipment: mixing bowl • wooden spoon metal spoon • baking sheet • cooling rack

Start cooking

1. Preheat the oven to 375°F (190°C).
2. Add the dry ingredients from the jar and combine with the butter and milk.
3. Mix in the candies.
4. Make the mixture into 20 balls of dough.
5. Place on the baking sheet and flatten the balls with the back of a spoon.
6. Put in the oven and bake for 15 mins. Take out and cool on a rack.

Craft-lover
Make a handy pincushion lid.

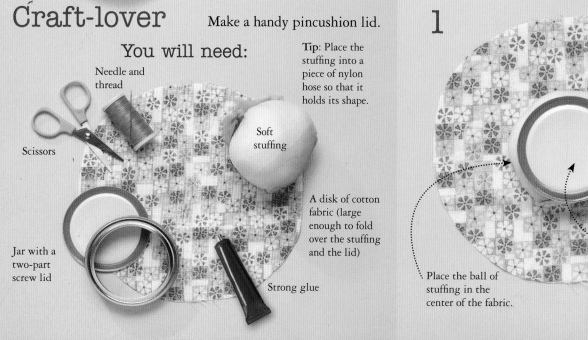

You will need:

Needle and thread

Scissors

Jar with a two-part screw lid

Soft stuffing

A disk of cotton fabric (large enough to fold over the stuffing and the lid)

Strong glue

Tip: Place the stuffing into a piece of nylon hose so that it holds its shape.

1

Place the ball of stuffing in the center of the fabric.

Put this part of the lid on top with the base facing out.

Doodler's kit
Make a giant pencil jar.

You will need: • brown kraft paper • pencil
• plate • black pen
• scissors • strong glue
• paper clip or other paper fastener

1
Draw around a plate to make a circle on the brown paper.

2
Cut out the paper circle.

Cut into the center.

Twist the paper to form a cone.

3
Check that the cone will fit the top of your jar.

Hold the cone in place with a clip while you glue it with strong glue. Leave the cone to dry.

4
Apply glue to the top of the lid, around the edge.

5
Hold the pencil top in position until the glue has dried.

Color in the tip of the pencil top with black pen.

Once the glue has dried, remove the lid. Fill the jar with gifts, then decorate.

2
Bring the fabric over the lid. Gather it up and stitch together.

3
Apply strong glue to the inside rim of the lid (not the screw part).

Push the cushion through the opening of the lid.

Stitch the fabric together tightly and secure the end of the thread.

4
Place the lid on top of the jar and screw it on tightly.

Let the glue dry, then open the jar and fill it with your gift.

Index